PROPER PASTIES
BILLY DEAKIN

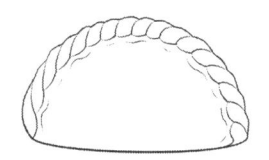

Published by Kernow Web

© Copyright Billy Deakin, 2013.
All rights reserved.

Acknowledgements

As many readers will know, this book was only made possible by the support and generosity of many people who backed my Kickstarter project. I wish to express my gratitude to everyone who pledged their support, however small. This book would not be a reality without your help.

In particular I'd like to thank, in no particular order, Simon Mosely, Meleri Pascoe, Hermit Games (Matthew Verran), Frank Blackwell, Oliver Ware, Skyler See, Dave Taub, Daniel Robins, Simon Boucher, Karen Macbeth, Rush, Marc Wylder, Michael La Posta, James Graham, Matthew Fernandes, Dave & Ella Wright, Jenny, Tim Stevens, Dr Buzz Palmer, and of course all of my family who helped out including my father, Cress, Fred, Tracy and Amba.

I really hope I've not missed anyone. For a full list of backers for the Kickstarter project, please see the "Wall of Thanks" page at ProperPasties.com

http://properpasties.com/wallofthanks.html

Disclaimer

I've done my best to keep the content of this book as accurate as possible. I've done considerable research, but there is no guarantee that all of the sources I used are 100% accurate. At the same time, some of what I've written is personal opinion, and not everyone will always agree with me.

I'm also not a professional writer. While I do spend an inordinate amount of time sat in front of a computer keyboard, I'm far more used to writing code in some obscure programming language, than in stringing actual words together into coherent sentences. For those reasons, I hope you'll forgive the odd spelling, punctuation or grammar mistake – it doesn't matter how much I proofread and check, there will always be a few that slip through. I'm also well aware that I sometimes start a sentence with "but", and use far too many exclamation marks!! But, I assume that most people reading this are far more interested in the content than in the technical accuracy of my writing. However, if that offends you in any way, please feel free to write me a letter, and I'll file it in the bin without reading it but at least it might make you feel better. Thanks for bearing with me, and I hope you enjoy reading the book, and trying the recipes!

Contents

Foreward	6
Introduction	8

Part 1 – Proper Pasties

A Brief History of the Pasty	11
The Pasty in Cornwall Today	17
The Cornish Pasty Association	19
Fifty Shades of Pasty (PGI Status)	20
Pastygate! (The Pasty Tax Scandal)	25
The World Pasty Championships	31
Pasties Around The World	36

Part 2 – Pasty Making

Ingredients	42
The Crimp	51
An Award Winning Pasty Recipe	61
Pasty Pie	64
Pastry Options	66
Other Pasty Recipes	74
Steak and Blue	77
Steak and Ale	78
Chilli Beef	80
Spiced Oxtail and Sweet Potato	82
Lamb and Mint	84

Pork and Sage	85
Cheese and Bacon	86
English Breakfast	87
Chicken and Mushroom	89
Chicken and Chorizo	91
Roasted Mediterranean Vegetable	92
Roasted Squash, Ricotta and Sage	94
Mushroom and Blue Cheese	96
Tricolore	98
Cheese, Leek and Onion	100
Cheese and Marmite	101
2 Course Pasties	102
Apple Pasties	108
Mince Pie Pasties	110
Appendices	
Top Pasty Shops in Cornwall	111
Tips for Making a Proper Pasty	112
Further Reading	114

Foreword

There are a few things which are guaranteed to warm the heart of any Cornishman or Cornishwoman; the sight of a deep red sunset from the top of Carn Brea on a clear summer's evening, the sound of waves crashing on the rocks far below while walking along a cliff path in a wintery gale, a sea of black and gold wearing fans (Trelawny's army) supporting their team at a Twickenham final, and the smell of a proper pasty straight from the oven!

The pasty is as iconically Cornish as the chough, the flag of St.Piran, or the sight of an abandoned engine house on a lonely cliff top. Steeped in history, and forever associated with Cornwall's mining heritage, the pasty has been a staple of the Cornish for centuries. It began as a utilitarian food for working men, yet today it's enjoyed as a gastronomic speciality of the region, not only by the locals but also by the millions of tourists who visit Cornwall each year.

So what makes a "proper pasty"? How did they evolve, and what made them so popular? And most importantly, how do you make a really good one?

This book attempts to answer these questions, gives you a glimpse of the pasty's history and an idea of why it became such an important and iconic meal, before showing you how to make delicious pasties in your own kitchen.

I hope you enjoy reading the book, but more importantly I hope you try the recipes and make some proper pasties yourself – there's nothing quite like the smell of pasties cooking in the oven. Despite what you might have heard, pastry isn't difficult to make, you don't need "cold hands" or a "light touch" you just need to follow a simple recipe and be accurate with your measuring.

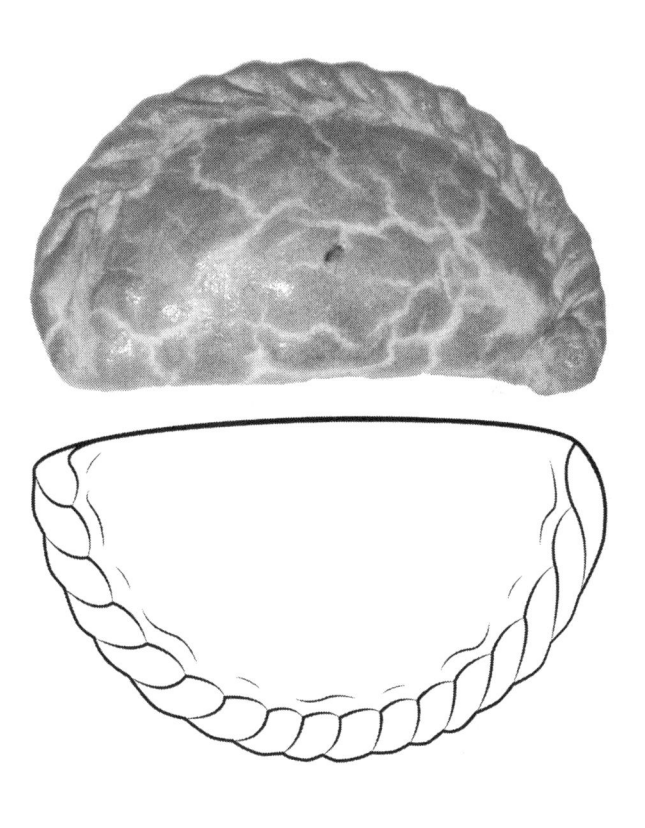

Introduction

"Makin' em, or eatin' em?"

Invariably, that's the first question everyone asks when they learn that I'm a "pasty champ". It's a question which always amuses me - I'm 6'1" and about 150lbs, so surely I don't look like I eat THAT many pasties, do I? At least it's an easy enough question to answer though, and people always seem genuinely interested to know more. The next question I get asked however isn't quite so easy to answer - "so what's the secret?"

I've been asked that question more times than I can count over the past 12 months since first picking up the title of Amateur Cornish Pasty World Champion - what's the secret to a great pasty? It's a question I've struggled to answer concisely, yet it's a question that I've thought about extensively and one I hope to address in this book.

Since a Cornish pasty is made in a specific way, using specific ingredients (more on that later!) you'd think that the differences between them really would be splitting hairs, yet I've had some cracking pasties in my time, as well as some absolute shockers! I've had pasties that melt in the mouth, and pasties that you need a hammer and chisel to get into. I've had pasties that tasted like they were crafted by the very hands of god, and pasties that tasted like a piece of warm cardboard. And I've seen pasties which wouldn't look out of place on display in the Louvre, while others look suspiciously like Jackson Pollock's number 5!

In this book, I aim to share my passion for the pasty, delve into their rich history and the reason that they are so important to the Cornish, and of course share my recipes, tips and techniques. In the process, I'm hopeful that I can answer the question, and teach you the secret to making a great pasty.

A Note About Illustrations

While writing this book it quickly became apparent that including photographs of all of the recipes would become very boring indeed – pasties do tend to look rather similar on the outside, no matter what delicious treats they are filled with or how skilfully they are crafted. So, while I have included some photographs in the book where it seemed to add to the text, I have purposely not included photographs of all of the pasty recipes. Instead, I've included some of my favourite snippets and quotes about food from other authors, cooks, and social narrators, which I hope you'll find at least as enlightening as any picture of a pasty!

PART 1
PROPER PASTIES

*"Cornish lads are fishermen,
and Cornish lads are miners too,
but when the fish and tin are gone
what are the Cornish boys to do?"*

A Brief History Of The Pasty

Fishing, and mining: Cornwall as a county (some would argue country!) was largely defined by these 2 great industries for centuries. Today, tourism is Cornwall's most important industry, making up almost a quarter of the economy and being responsible for 1 in 5 jobs in the county, but you don't need to go very far back in time to find fishing and mining as the dominant industries, with both being immensely important to the Cornish economy.

Fishing, in particular pilchard fishing, had long been important for the Cornish people, and up until around 1700 it was as important an industry as mining to the Cornish economy. It was, however, the start of the industrial revolution which put Cornwall firmly on the map, since with the dawn of the age of steam the miners could dig deeper and increase yields. The skill and ingenuity of Cornish miners and engineers enabled the development of techniques to massively increase yields, and the Cornish became world renowned for their mining expertise. Cornwall had an abundance of copper and tin ore, and the Cornish miners became experts at extracting it, putting Cornwall firmly on the map as the world's biggest tin mining industry, and a vital component of the UK's economy. In fact, the ore was so abundant that in the 1720s the Chacewater-Gwennap mining district near Redruth was dubbed "The richest square mile on earth".

Ruins of the Poldice mine in Gwennap,
once part of the "richest square mile on earth"

Wheal Busy, now nothing more than a few old ruins just up the road from where I grew up, lies in that district and is just one example of how successful the Cornish miners were. During its lifetime, that mine produced over 100,000 tons of copper ore and 27,000 tons of arsenic.

And of course, the Cornish landscape is covered in the remains of countless mines, crumbling towers that stand as memorials to that once proud industry.

But now the fish and tin are gone. The quote at the start of this chapter is from a Cornish folk song called *Cornish Lads* by Roger Bryant. The line was poignantly painted on the outside wall of South Crofty mine, soon after it closed in 1998. The closure marked the end of a 400 year history of the mine, and a 4000 year history of mining in the area, since South Crofty was the very last working mine in Cornwall.

Of course, nothing lasts forever and while many people were, and still are, sad about the decline and eventual collapse of the mining industry, it should also be remembered that it left a lasting heritage. Go anywhere in the world today where they mine tin or copper, and you'll find Cornish miners and a Cornish influence. As the old saying goes - "anywhere you find a hole, you'll find a Cousin Jack" (Cornish person). From Australia to Mexico, Canada to Brazil, and South Africa to New Zealand - there are mines all over the world, with communities of Cornish descent built up around them. They took their mining expertise, they took their language and place names (just check the map of any mining area and you'll find plenty of Redruths and Cambornes!) and they took their music, but most importantly they took their food - saffron buns, cream teas, and pasties!

Pasty /ˈpæsti/ *n.* (*pl.* **-ies**) a pastry case with a sweet or savoury filling, baked without a dish to shape it.

The dictionary definition does nothing to convey the brilliance in design or exquisite character of this iconic dish, or why it's so loved both within Cornwall and elsewhere. There are many reasons to love the pasty - the taste, the smell, that rush of hot steam that bursts out when you take your first bite! But the real reason for the pasty's popularity is mostly utilitarian - they are practical.

A miner (or a farmer or fisherman for that matter) can take a pasty, wrapped in linen, to work with them and not only will it still be fresh and warm when they come to eat it, but tucked into a coat pocket it will keep them warm in the meantime! They are the perfect "portable meal", coming in their own packaging and leaving nothing to waste. As Mary Wright puts in in her book *Cornish Treats*, "pasties provided a complete and easily portable meal for miners on long shifts underground".

Now let's clear one thing up before we go any further - contrary to what you might have heard, the Cornish tin miners didn't invent the pasty. While there's evidence of mining in Cornwall dating back to the early Bronze age, approximately 2150 BC, mining's true heyday in Cornwall was in the 19th Century and there is evidence of pasty recipes dating back several hundred years before that. It was however mining which popularised the pasty, out of necessity, and to imagine the pasty today without Cornwall's mining heritage would be impossible. As Stephen Hall puts it so well in *The Cornish Pasty*, "The pasty was the answer to every 19th century Cornish miner's prayer. It had been waiting in the wings for hundreds of years; a solution in search of a problem: an invention yearning for an application."

In fact, many of the earliest known recipes for pasties used venison, as pasties were then regarded as a luxury dish, fit to be served up at the grandest of banquets. Exactly when and where these early pasties were first adopted as a worker's meal for miners is unknown, but during the 17th and 18th century the pasty became more and more popular as the Cornish miners discovered not only their practicality, but also the sheer satisfaction of eating a pasty.

Today, the Cornish pasty is worth over £65 million per year to the Cornish economy, and quite aside from the pasties eaten within Cornwall, almost 2 million are exported each week proving the pasty's immense popularity. There can be few people in Cornwall who don't have a pasty for lunch or tea on a regular basis, and I challenge anyone to find me a true Cornishman who hasn't had a pasty for breakfast at least once (they are ideal as a "recovery breakfast" after a late night with one too many Doom Bars, or Betty Stogs - so I'm told!)

So you see, the dictionary definition really doesn't do the pasty justice. I much prefer Angus Murdoch's description, as penned in *Cornwall's Legacy to American Mining, Part III* (1970):

Pasty /ˈpæsti/ *n.* "a portable beef stew, folded into a purse of a pie dough and baked to a rich golden brown. No one but a cousin Jenny could do a proper job."

A selection of hand crafted entries, on display in the judging area at the 2013 World Pasty Championships

The Pasty in Cornwall Today

W. Somerset Maugham once wrote that "if you want to eat well in England, you should eat three breakfasts". I suspect that if he ever visited Cornwall, that famous line could well have been very different!

The Cornish are proud of our pasties, and rightly so. We've already seen how important the pasty was historically, and how they have been taken around the world by the Cornish miners, but now that the fish and tin are gone why is the pasty still so popular? Of course, it's not just popular in Cornwall. Over 100 million pasties are exported from Cornwall every year, and that number is increasing (according to Emma Mansfield's *The Little Book Of The Pasty* that's enough to stretch from Land's End to John O"Groats 18 times!)

Why is the Cornish pasty so popular? The reason dear reader, of course, is that they taste "bleddy 'ansum"!

At the Glastonbury Festival this year I counted not one, not two, not even three but four Cornish pasty vendors (there could well have been more, but the festival is massive and it's hard to count after your fourth pint of cider!) Glastonbury of course isn't in Cornwall, it's in Somerset, so 4 traders selling nothing but Cornish pasties for the entire week struck me as evidence for the pasty's enduring popularity (and of course it's the perfect festival food. You need 2 hands to eat a bag of chips, but with a pasty in one hand you have an entire hand free for holding a pint of cider!)

Cornish pasty companies have expanded all over the UK. At the time of writing, Pasty Presto's website lists 27 pasty shops, as far away as Birmingham and Guernsey. The West Cornwall Pasty Company lists 73, including one in Glasgow, which I assume has to be the current record in the UK.

There are even pasty shops in other countries, like this one in California, USA

Of course, if you want the real deal you need to ignore these mass produced pasties (even though some of them aren't too bad) and come to a proper pasty shop here in Cornwall. The point however, is that pasties are big business. In fact, it's estimated that 13,000 jobs in Cornwall rely on the pasty trade, and a survey by the South West tourism board found that one of the top three reasons people visit Cornwall is for the food, and that the pasty is the food most associated with Cornwall (I'm not sure how much they spent on that research, but I could have told them that for free!

The Cornish Pasty Association

In 2002, a group of pasty makers in Cornwall got together to form the Cornish Pasty Association (CPA) in order to protect the quality and reputation of this important product, and the pasty's contribution to the Cornish economy. The CPA consists of more than 50 pasty producers who together employ over 1,800 people directly involved in pasty production in the county.

One of the primary goals of the Cornish Pasty Association, was to safeguard the heritage of the Cornish pasty, the future of the industry, and the reputation of the product. At the time, many companies were producing and selling "Cornish pasties" that were not made in Cornwall, and not made to a traditional recipe. For those reasons, the CPA worked hard to obtain Protected Geographic Indication (PGI) status for the Cornish Pasty.

In 2011, it was finally announced that the Cornish pasty had been granted PGI status, the same protection enjoyed by other world renowned regional produce such as Parma ham, Champagne and Stilton cheese. This legal protection means that now, only pasty makers based in Cornwall and baking their pasties in a traditional manner to a traditional recipe are allowed to label their products as Cornish pasties.

Fifty Shades of Pasty

Nothing is ever black and white. In my opinion, anything said by a politician or a lawyer should be taken with a good pinch of salt. When it comes to European legislation (such as PGI status) many politicians and lawyers are involved, so you can be pretty sure that there are some grey areas, and a whole shovel full of salt may be needed.

On the face of it, PGI status for the Cornish pasty seems like a good thing. It makes logical sense to most people that a proper Cornish pasty should be made in Cornwall. It recognises the Cornish pasty as something of significance; a unique product with a heritage worth protecting. And the PGI status prevents "rip offs" being made elsewhere at a cut price and so protects businesses and workers here in the county... or does it?

The CPA website claims that they were formed in 2002 to "protect the quality and the reputation of the Cornish pasty and to stop consumers being misled by pasty makers who trade off the value of the name without producing a genuine product." Certainly that sounds like a worthwhile cause, but does the PGI status really do that?

You see, the PGI status doesn't really "protect the quality" of the pasty in my opinion. The PGI specification (available freely online at the UK government web site, and linked to from the appendix) mentions no requirements for quality, other than to say that Cornish pasties must be free from artificial colours, flavours or preservatives. They also state that the meat content must be no less than 12½%, that the vegetable content must be no less than 25%, and that the filling must be beef, potato, swede, onion and seasoning.

Nowhere does it mention the quality or provenance of those ingredients. In fact, it clearly states that either diced or minced beef can be used. Why would they do that, if it's clear to most people that using minced beef creates an inferior product, when the goal of the CPA in petitioning for PGI status was to "protect the quality and reputation of the Cornish pasty"? The reason, it seems, is financial. You see, some big producers such as Ginsters sell millions of their mass produced products each year in supermarkets and filling stations all over the country, and in making their low price point product they use minced beef. They are also members of the CPA!

> *"Having the [PGI] status sounds nice for Cornish suppliers, but in fact it opens the doors for a lot of cheap imitations."*
>
> - Tim Pointer, Pengenna Pasties, Bude

So it seems clear that while the Cornish pasty's PGI status is a good thing in general, the idea that it was done purely to protect the heritage, integrity and quality of the pasty is shady at best. More than likely, the primary reason for the CPA pushing for PGI status was to protect the business interests of its members, and that's fair enough... but it gets worse!

There is one seemingly insignificant line on page 2 of the specification which reads:

"On assembling Cornish Pasties, the pasties are 'D' shaped and pastry edges are crimped either by hand or mechanically to one side, and never on top."

The "or mechanically" part is clearly there to protect the interests of the big mass producers but that's not the issue, the issue is the statement that the crimp must be on the side and "never on top". You see, some Cornish people have been crimping their pasties on the side for hundreds of years... and some have been crimping on top for just as long! Tim Pointer of Pengenna Pasties in Bude had this to say:

"It is a bit of a thorn in our side as our pasties are the wrong shape to qualify to be advertised as Cornish pasties. Ours have a small crimp on top, the PGI description is for Cornish Pasties to have a large side crimp."

There are small, artisan producers in Cornwall who have been making and selling their pasties to a traditional recipe for generations, and crimping them on the top.

Due to the PGI specification they are no longer allowed to legally sell their pasties as "Cornish pasties" despite the fact that they are made in Cornwall, to a traditional Cornish recipe, by second or third generation pasty makers. These small businesses are not allowed to call their pasties "Cornish pasties", even though they are making a high quality product, in the traditional way – exactly what the CPA claims to be trying to protect. Doesn't seem right does it, not when a big company can mass produce a mince filled product wrapped in plastic, sold from a refrigerator in a filling station, and yet still be allowed to call them Cornish pasties because they are crimped on the side!

Please don't get me wrong, I'm not against the CPA. I think they do a lot of good and certainly some of the CPA members make fantastic pasties. Neither do I think the PGI status of the Cornish pasty is bad in itself, on the contrary I believe it does offer rightful protection to a unique product. I do however feel that, like most things in life, the argument for and against isn't clear cut and I wanted to offer the reader both sides. Certainly the way the PGI specification was laid out appears to have been done largely to favour the big mass producers, rather than to simply protect the heritage and quality of a unique regional product. For businesses such as the Samworth Brothers, who amongst many other business interests own Ginsters with their fleet of 150 delivery vehicles shipping their plastic wrapped wares to motorway services all over the country, the PGI status seems to be a massive triumph – but that's hardly surprising since they are founder members of the CPA. While Ginsters itself is based in Cornwall, the parent company of Samworth Brothers has its registered office in Leicestershire, so it's not even as if all the money from their substantial sales (listed as over £500 million per year in a recent Sunday Times list of top UK companies) is staying in the Cornish economy. As to whether or not the PGI status of the Cornish pasty, or the CPA themselves for that matter, are a good or bad thing for the Cornish pasty, or for Cornwall in general, I'll leave that for you, dear reader, to decide for yourself.

Left: A beautiful looking hand made pasty, but since it's crimped on top it can't legally be sold as a "Cornish pasty".

Right: This plastic wrapped, mince filled abomination *can* legally be sold as a Cornish pasty due to the way the PGI specification has been laid out.

Pastygate
The Pasty Tax Scandal

"You'll never stop the British people laughing... though they did get bleddy close with that poll tax thing" - Jethro

You'll never stop the Cornish people laughing either... but they did get bleddy close with the pasty tax!

In the spring of 2012 the Chancellor of the Exchequer, Conservative MP George Osborne, announced in the annual budget that the rules governing VAT on "hot takeaway food" would be changed, to make it payable where it had previously been exempt. Of course, this would mean a massive increase in the cost of pasties, and it became a major political controversy, dubbed in at least one newspaper as "Pastygate".

With any controversial legislation, there will of course be people who are passionate on both sides of the argument. The coalition government's stance was that pasties, and other baked goods which were sold straight from the oven, had been exempt from VAT due to a loophole which they intended to close in order to end "anomalies" and to "level the playing field" between retailers. Foods such as fish and chips or pizza, which are cooked and sold hot, always qualified for VAT. Pasties, and other baked goods such as sausage rolls were exempt since they were not necessarily eaten hot – they are often taken away and eaten later in the day, or reheated at home.

In his budget speech, Osborne stated that he wanted to create a level playing field by imposing the tax on bakeries and supermarkets selling hot food to bring them in line with fast-food outlets which were already paying VAT. His suggestion was that any food bought at higher than "ambient temperature" should require VAT to be paid. Clearly the man has never worked in a bakery or a pasty shop; did he really expect customers to pay one price for a cold pasty, and another for a warm one from the same shop? What about the customer who wants to buy a tax-exempt cold pasty to eat later in the day, but the only ones the shop has left are straight from the oven? Should the customer wait for 30 minutes before making his purchase, or pay an extra 20%?

The idea that it "levelled the playing field" with fast food outlets never really made sense either. I don't know about you, but I've never bought fish and chips and then taken it away to eat cold for my lunch a few hours later, have you?

Needless to say, the vast majority of Cornish folk were very much against George Osborne's plans and there was a backlash. A petition against the tax, delivered to Downing Street in April 2012, boasted over half a million signatures, while claims that the government "are out of touch with ordinary hard working people" were levied against David Cameron and his colleagues.

Of course, being a politician, Cameron responded in the

way he knows best – by apparently lying and making himself look even more of a prat than usual (rather a difficult task it has to be said!). At a press conference for the London Olympics, Cameron said, "I am a pasty eater myself. I go to Cornwall on holiday. I love a hot pasty. I think the last one I bought was from the Cornwall Pasty Company. I seem to remember I was in Leeds station at the time and the choice was whether to have one of their small ones or large ones, and I have a feeling I opted for the large one and very good it was too."

The first thing that strikes me from that statement is, why is he saying he goes to Cornwall for his holidays and then talking about buying a pasty in Leeds? Surely, as Prime Minister, his geography of the UK isn't THAT bad?!?

I suspect he soon regretted mentioning Leeds at all however, since the next day several journalists had discovered that the West Cornwall Pasty Company outlet at Leeds station had closed down in 2007! So I guess he was either lying, or he's a very irregular pasty eater – about one every 5 years!

If politicians have a reputation for being, shall we say "flexible with the truth", they are also known for taking "donations" from people and organisations who might benefit from their decision making. And sure enough, it would only be a matter of weeks before another embarrassing story hit the headlines about the Conservatives. It turned out that they had received a donation of £100,000 from Mark Samworth, a director of Samworth Brothers which own and operate Ginsters. Ginsters of course are the UK's biggest supplier of cold pasties, which would continue to be tax exempt under the new laws.

Karl Turner, Labour MP said, "This smells worse than a mouldy pasty. Just days after George Osborne slapped a massive tax hike on 'hot' pies, the Tories got a six-figure donation from someone who makes 'cold' snacks. This could reheat David Cameron's cash-for-policies scandal."

In defence of the donation, a statement from Samworth Brothers read that "The donation was made in a personal capacity and has no connection to the business". Well fair enough then, I guess it must have just been a complete coincidence that a director of the UK's biggest supplier of cold pasties made a large cash donation to the government just weeks after a tax was imposed on hot pasties which would presumably negatively impact their competitors... move along people, nothing to see here!

U-turn

After protests, marches and petitions against the proposed pasty tax, the government altered the definition of what is considered a "hot" pasty to allow for a reversal of its controversial plans.

The amendment allowed for pasties which were sold as they were cooling down (but not kept hot in a special cabinet) to continue to be exempt from VAT.

This was of course welcome news, for pasty sellers and customers alike. While a pasty that was kept artificially warm in a heated cabinet or on a hot plate would incur VAT, a hot pasty straight from the oven would not. Many pasty shops stated that they would make small changes to allow their customers to avoid the tax, mostly by cooking smaller batches more often to reduce the need for using a heated cabinet.

George Eustice, Conservative MP for Camborne and Redruth was delighted with the u-turn, stating that "this is very good news. It is everything we and the industry have asked for." And in fact, this ruling does indeed meet with the originally stated targets of the tax – to force supermarkets onto a more level playing field with smaller businesses. If a supermarket has a cabinet full of hot pasties, they will incur 20% VAT. On the other hand, a small pasty shop down the road, selling their pasties straight from the oven, will not.

Of course, not everyone was happy. Labour were quick to state that the u-turn on pasty tax, combined with a change to a proposed tax on static caravans, would add £110 million to the government's deficit. For the Cornish however, and pasty lovers across the land, the u-turn was a triumph. Well done Trelawny's army – proper job!

"The Cornish people have won and there will be dancing in streets from Land's End to the Tamar as people hear that the Government has dropped their plans to clobber local people and local businesses with this tax."

- Stephen Gilbert, Liberal Democrat MP

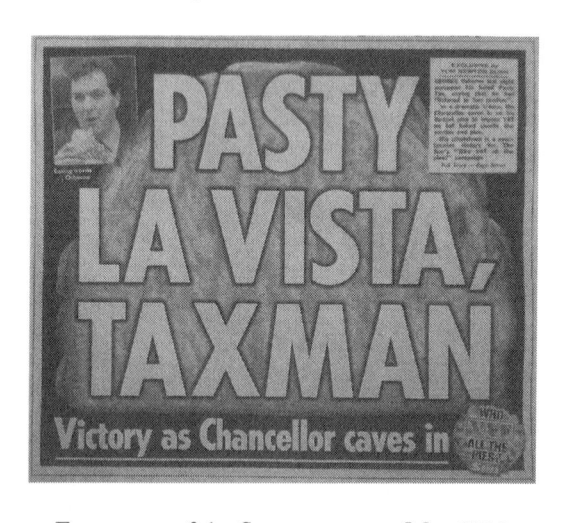

Front page of the Sun newspaper, May 2012

The World Pasty Championships

In 2012, the Eden Project teamed up with the Cornish Pasty Association to host the inaugural World Pasty Championships. The event attracted over 100 entries, not only from Cornwall but from as far afield as the USA. Awards were given to both professional and amateur pasty makers, competing in two categories - traditional Cornish (which had to comply with PGI specifications) and an open category which could include any savoury filling.

I decided to enter for fun, and though I hoped to place well I was surprised when I won first place, taking the title of Amateur Cornish Pasty World Champion. Even more of a surprise however was what a great event Eden put on. The day was packed with music and dance, workshops, pasty trivia, comedy, children's activities and more with highlights including the hilarious Kernow King, and the dulcet tones of the Aberfal Oggymen. It was a real celebration of the pasty and of Cornishness, and the day ended with an awards ceremony dubbed the "Oggy Oscars".

I was unable to attend the awards ceremony (not knowing I had won, my wife and I had gone home by that point to walk the dog!) but it turns out there was some controversy. The winner of the professional category was the aptly named Graham Cornish. The controversy however was that he worked for Ginsters!

Needless to say, it wasn't a Ginster's "pasty" that won (sorry but I had to put that in quotation marks, I just can't bring myself to call their products pasties!) rather he had made it at home, by hand, to his own recipe. People however put 2 and 2 together, made 5 and started assuming that it was a fix, and that it was actually a Ginster's pasty which had won.

Eden of course were quick to make it clear that despite working for Ginsters, the pasty Graham had entered had been made by hand, himself, using his own recipe but that didn't stop a plethora of negative comments on Facebook and blogs over the coming days such as "Ginsters do not make pasties! Whichever fool awarded Ginsters these awards must be ashamed with themselves", "Grandmother would be turning in her grave. Disgusting results!" and even "They are to Cornish pasties what the Taliban are to world peace." Even I think that third one is a bit over the top, but it shows how passionate some people are about their beloved pasties!

Clearly this wasn't the PR that Eden, or the CPA, wanted and so they quickly began work on making changes to the rules to avoid this sort of controversy in the future.

Based on that, and the experience they had gained from running the first competition, the Eden Project came back with a bigger and better pasty championships in 2013, with several new categories. Firstly a new children's category was introduced, and secondly a "company" category was added, with rules stipulating that "These pasties must be produced to exactly the same recipe and method and in the same place as the Cornish pasty that your business sells to the public." This rule would prevent any winning pasty being misrepresented as one from a commercial producer, if it wasn't what they actually sold.

For myself, going back to defend my title added a new challenge. Not only was there some expectation (in 2012 I was just entering for fun, now I was trying to prove it wasn't a fluke) but also there was media attention to deal with. In the weeks running up to the event, I did a number of radio and newspaper interviews, while Cornwall Today came to cook pasties with me at my home, running a 3 page spread. The Guardian even requested a recipe from me which they published. It was at this point that I realised that if I was to win again, I could probably write a book. That of course added even more pressure – the competition had heated up, and now I was determined to win!

On the morning of the 2013 championships I was tired and a little stressed. I'd spent most of the previous day at the Eden Project being filmed making pasties and doing interviews for the evening news, with camera crews from BBC Spotlight and ITV Westcountry. I rushed home, straight into the kitchen to begin making pasties which I'd be entering the following day. Another interview (this time for Radio 5 Live) and I eventually finished baking around 11pm. I wasn't as happy with the pasties as I'd have liked, I knew I'd rushed them and the crimping wasn't as neat as usual but I was too tired to start over so they had to do.

After handing the pasties over on arrival at Eden the next morning, I tried to relax and enjoy the day's entertainment, but despite there being a packed day of music, dance, comedy and more, it felt like an awfully long time until the awards ceremony. This time we had put the dogs into kennels for the day so we didn't have to rush home, and it turned out to be the right decision; I was successful in defending my title despite there being many more entries than the previous year, and despite not being 100% happy with my late night baking.

I decided that once could have been a fluke, but to win the title 2 years running proved that I could indeed make a proper pasty! I knew then that I had to write my book, and started to wonder if I could do the hat trick and win it three years running...

Graham Cornish, who had won the professional title the year before, decided not to enter a pasty himself, but his 2 children both picked up prizes in the kid's category which was nice to see – he might work for Ginsters, but he can clearly make a proper pasty in his own kitchen and is teaching his kids to do the same – proper job!

Once again Eden had hosted a fantastic event, bigger and better than the year before, and this time with no "embarrassing" confusion over any of the winning pasties!

The winners of the 2 company categories were Pasty Presto, and The Chough Bakery and I was particularly pleased that Brian Etherington Meat Company had picked up a third place – they are just down the road from me, and that happened to be where I bought the beef that I used in my own pasties for the competition.

The 2013 World Pasty Championships were certainly bigger and better than 2012, so I wonder what Eden have in store for next year? One thing is for sure, you now have the previous winning recipe in your hands, so the question is, will YOU be collecting a trophy at next year's *oggy oscars*?

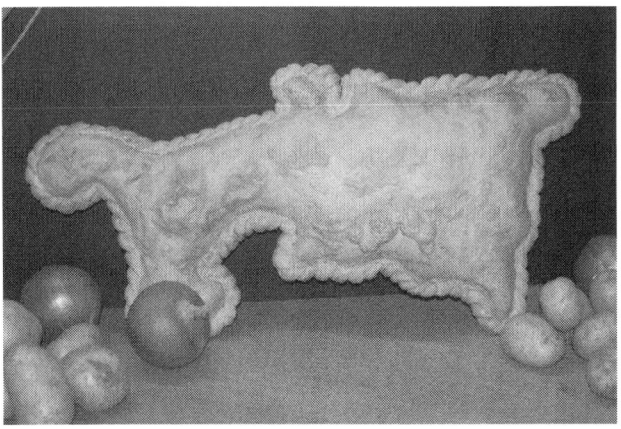

A Cornwall shaped giant pasty at the 2013 championships

Pasties Around The World

"Where there's a mine or a hole in the ground
That's what I'm heading for that's where I'm bound
Look for me under the lode or inside the vein,
Where the copper, the clay, where the arsenic and tin
Run in your blood they get under your skin
I'm leaving the county behind and I'm not coming back
So follow me down Cousin Jack."

- Cousin Jack, Show Of Hands

The old saying goes that, "Wherever there's a hole in the ground, you'll find a Cousin Jack at the bottom of 'un". A Cousin Jack, or Cousin Jenny, simply means a Cornishman or Cornishwoman. The nickname dates back to a time when it was common to greet one another in Cornwall as "cousin", and Jack and Jenny were at that time the most common names.

The "hole in the ground" of course relates to mining, and as we saw in a previous chapter, the Cornish exported their mining skills all over the world. Where there's copper, tin, or arsenic in the ground you'll be sure to find Cousin Jacks, and Cousin Jennys. And where you find Cousin Jacks and Cousin Jennys, you find pasties!

The extent of the Cornish diaspora runs wide, with Cornish communities in mining areas of the United

States, Canada, Australia, Mexico, New Zealand and South Africa. It's estimated that as the local mining industry was in decline between 1861 and 1901 some 250,000 Cornish emigrated, taking their mining skills and their pasty recipes with them.

Where the Cornish settled they had a dramatic effect on the local area, building tight knit communities and keeping Cornish traditions alive. In Moonta, South Australia, the descendants of those immigrants are so numerous that they host the World's largest annual Cornish festival – Kernewek Lowender (Cornish happiness) which attracts tens of thousands of visitors each year.

It's estimated that 20% of the population of South Australia have a Cornish heritage (more than the number living here in Cornwall!) In the United States there's an estimated 2 million people with Cornish heritage, mostly centred around the mining areas such as Butte in Montanna, and the Upper Peninsula of Michigan. And in all the places that the Cousin Jacks and Cousin Jennys settled, they are as proud of their Cornish heritage and especially the pasty as any native Cornish ever are!

Like any stranger in a foreign land, the Cornish had to adapt to different climates and different local resources. That has led to some subtle differences in pasties around the world, such as the insistence of people in the UP of Michigan (known as "Yoopers" - UP, for Upper

Peninsula) of eating their pasties with a dollop of ketchup, while pasties in Butte, Montana, are generally served smothered in gravy!

It's not just condiments either, differences in fillings, crust and crimping are also noticeable from place to place. Taking Butte again as an example: if you order a pasty there what you'll get will generally be round and suspiciously 'pie' looking (especially when it's smothered in gravy, or served with a jug of gravy on the side). Residents of Butte insist that they are pasties however, and once you break through the odd looking crust you'll certainly see evidence of pasty heritage – beef, onion, potato and rutabaga (the word that most Americans use for swede, more on that later!). It certainly smells and tastes like a pasty, and there's no doubting the Cornish heritage of the good people of Butte, though quite why they have evolved their pasties in such a way is a mystery.

Typical Butte pasty served with gravy on the side!

Aside from pasties around the world with a Cornish heritage, there are pasty-like foods in the cuisines of many countries which developed independently. Calzones from Italy, Empanadas from Mexico, Bierock from Germany, Salteñas from Argentina – the list goes on and on. It seems that wrapping meat and vegetables in some sort of crust is just a "good idea" that lots of different cultures hit upon to a greater or lesser extent.

There's no doubt that some of the pasty-like foods around the world were influenced by the pasty to some degree (The Mexican "paste" for example even sounds like "pasty") however, it's just as clear that others were not. Food such as the Italian calzone for example appear to have developed entirely independently from the pasty.

This might look like a box of Cornish pasties, but in fact these are Argentinian "empanadas salteñas". Dating back to the early nineteenth century, there can be little doubt that these are heavily influenced by the Cornish pasty, taken to to Argentina by European settlers.

PART 2
PASTY MAKING

HOW TO MAKE AN AWARD WINNING CORNISH PASTY

Ingredients

"To get the best flavour you need to use the best ingredients. Use local produce if you can. At the end of the day simplicity is the key." - Michel Roux Snr.

There are only a handful of key ingredients in a proper pasty, so getting them right is essential, because there's nowhere to hide. In the introduction to this book I said that one of the questions I get asked the most is, "What's the secret to your pasties?". Well, I guess the closest there is to a "secret" is using the best quality ingredients. You'll struggle to make a great pasty with cheap supermarket beef, budget flour, and a poor choice of potato variety. On the other hand, take the time and effort to buy good quality beef from your local butcher, invest in decent flour, and use fresh local vegetables and you really will notice the difference.

They say that "you are what you eat" and a pasty can only be as good as the ingredients used to make it. Yes, you might pay slightly more for higher quality, local produce. However, not only will it taste great, but you'll also be giving your money to the local economy rather than shareholders in a big multinational supermarket, reducing your carbon footprint by avoiding unnecessary food miles, and probably eating more nutritious food with less chemicals in it – that has to be a win-win situation if ever I heard one.

Flour

I once had a girlfriend whose mother made pasties with a crust so hard I was often tempted to take a hammer and chisel with me when invited round for dinner (don't worry I never actually did, I suspect that it might have been somewhat frowned upon!). While there are several things which can cause tough pastry, most obviously using too much water and overworking it, I'm sure that a big part of the problem was her insistence on using cheap "value" flour from the supermarket.

The crust is what defines a pasty. It's such an important part of a pasty that it's essential to get it right, not only so that it does its structural job of holding its shape and encasing the filling, but also so that it tastes good. To get the texture right and the taste great, you need to buy decent flour.

Many people suggest using strong flour (bread flour) for pasties. The logic being that, unlike a pie, a pasty needs high structural integrity so it can be eaten in the hand without falling apart. The high gluten content in strong flour means that the pasty does firm up and hold its shape extremely well. This also has the added benefit of making the pastry slightly easier to roll out and crimp, but in my opinion that is at the expense of texture. I feel that pastry made with strong flour is slightly chewy, and that there is no need: if you use plain flour and do it properly, not only will the crimping be easy, but the cooked crust will hold its shape even when eaten in the hand, and it will taste great and crumble nicely in the mouth.

So I use plain white flour for my pasty pastry, and I always buy good quality flour from a reputable brand. There are slight differences between brands, particularly with regards to how much water they will absorb, so I would suggest that when you find a brand you like you stick with it.

There is however a time when I use strong flour, and that is for a wholemeal crust. Wholemeal flour has a lower gluten content than white flour, so I would normally use a strong wholemeal flour (often branded as wholemeal bread flour) or use normal wholemeal flour mixed with strong white flour in a 2 to 1 ratio. Bear in mind that a wholemeal pastry will absorb more water than white, and that it can be worked a little more.

Meat

Whatever type of meat you're using in a pasty, I highly recommend buying from a good local butcher. Very rarely does any supermarket meat compare to the quality and flavour of meat from a good butcher, and of course with a butcher there are so many other advantages (like being able to get bones for stock, or for the dogs!)

For a Cornish pasty of course we want beef, and the best cut to use is skirt. Beef skirt is a cut from the plate, which is a prime cut from the underside of the cow (behind the brisket). It's an incredibly versatile and under used cut of beef with great texture and lots of flavour. It's not too expensive, and since it can be used in so many ways (everything from long, slow braising to fast stir frying if treated properly) I always buy a good amount and freeze what I don't use. If you're in Cornwall, some butchers will actually label skirt as "pasty meat" or "pasty beef", but elsewhere it will be called skirt, or possibly plate.

If you can't get skirt for any reason, you could use flank or chuck.

Potatoes

Ideally you want to choose a potato variety that will be firm enough to maintain their consistency during the long cooking. There's nothing worse than biting into a pasty and finding it filled with a soggy mush (on that note, using minced beef in a pasty should, in my opinion, be a criminal offence!!)

So it's the firm, waxy varieties of potato that work best. Maris Piper, Wilja, Charlotte, Jersey Royals etc. will all do the job. Of course, Cornish new potatoes work perfectly when in season. Just avoid floury varieties such as King Edwards and Roosters as they will tend to become overly soft during cooking.

Swede (did someone say turnip?)

I have to be honest, I've been dreading writing this section of the book, since this is a subject which can almost cause riots in Cornwall – what to call that large, purple, bulbous root vegetable with the yellow flesh?

The scientific (Latin) name is *Brassica napobrassica* (although even that is contestable with some authorities listing it as *Brassica napus subsp. rapifera*) but the common names include **swede** (short for Swedish turnip), **yellow turnip, turnip, neep** (from the Old English *næp*, commonly used in Scotland), **rutabaga** (commonly used in the USA) and even lesser known and quite adorable colloquial names such as **baigie, tumshie, snadgers, snaggers** and **narkies**!

The main cause of confusion is that the majority of the UK, including many people in Cornwall, use the term swede, while at the same time there are lots of Cornish people who insist on the term turnip, especially when referring to pasty ingredients.

Now, calling them turnips certainly isn't wrong. They are, after all, a species of turnip (they originated as a cross between a white turnip and a cabbage). However, the word turnip is commonly used throughout the UK and most of the English speaking world to refer to the white turnip (*Brassica rapa rapa*), often known as the Milan turnip, and also referred to as the "true turnip" by a number of sources, including the Encyclopedia Brittanica, and the Merriam-Webster dictionary.

Almost every supermarket, greengrocer, cook book and restaurant menu uses the term "swede" to refer to the Swedish (yellow) turnip (which is what we use in pasties), and "turnip" to refer to the Milan (white) turnip... except, when talking about pasties in Cornwall you'll often see turnip used to refer to the Swedish turnip!

Confused yet? Well I'm not surprised. In fact, the linguistic quirks that surround this vegetable are so entrenched that when the European PGI status was awarded to the Cornish pasty in 2011, special consideration was given to it. Under European law, genuine Cornish pasties can be advertised as containing "turnip" so long as that "turnip" is actually swede (they can of course also be advertised as containing "swede"). However, they cannot be sold if they contain "turnip" (meaning Milan or white turnip)!

Swede /ˈswēd/ *n.* (*pl.* -s)
1. a Eurasian plant, *Brassica napus* (or *B. napobrassica*), cultivated for its bulbous edible root, which is used as a vegetable and as cattle fodder: family *Brassicaceae* (crucifers)
2. the root of this plant
[From its introduction from Sweden.]

Now, at the risk of offending some of my readers I've decided to use the term swede throughout the recipes in this book, purely for the sake of brevity and simplicity. I know that many will feel this is "plain wrong" (I've been told so to my face and via email several times in heated and colourful language, in fact I thought a fight was going to break out on one occasion!) but equally, if I use the word turnip there are lots of people who would complain, and I feel it would cause even more confusion. An argument that I've heard on several occasions is that the word swede is "simply a slang term for Swedish turnip". While the gist of that argument is correct (that is the origin of the word) it shows a lack of understanding of the evolution of language. Languages aren't static, they are constantly evolving and it would be hard to make a claim that a word, such as swede, which can be traced back to 1781-2 and is listed in all the major English dictionaries, is "just a slang term"! It is an abbreviation, but one that has been in popular use for so long that it's now considered as a word in it's own right. Claiming that it's just a slang term would be like saying "vitamin" is just a slang term, as technically it's short for vital amine, or that "car" is slang since it's a shortened form of carriage.

Now please don't think I'm trying to say that swede is the "correct" word to use, or that anyone who uses the word turnip is wrong. On the contrary, I firmly believe that anyone who claims that one or the other is correct while the other is wrong merely betrays their own etymological ignorance. I'm simply choosing to use the word swede in this book to avoid confusion.

The simple fact dear reader, is that when you are out shopping for ingredients you're far more likely to see these beautiful root vegetables labelled as swedes than as turnips and therefore it would be unfair on you if I called them anything else. If you take offence at that, please forgive me... and if you're reading this on the other side of the Atlantic, ignore everything I just said and use rutabaga!!

Left: The bigger, dark purple coloured swede (Swedish turnip) with its distinctive yellow flesh. Right: The small, pink and white turnip (Milan turnip) with bitter tasting white flesh.

Everything else

White onions, black pepper (and also a little white pepper!), salt, butter... all the rest of the ingredients are nice and simple. Don't stress about ingredients though. If you can't get the cut of beef you want, don't have time to visit your local butcher and have to use supermarket beef, or don't know what variety of potato you happen to have in your kitchen just use what you have – cooking is supposed to be fun, so use what you have or what you can get and enjoy the process.

If using good quality ingredients is half of "the secret" to making a great pasty, then the other half has to be passion, and you can't be passionate if you're stressed. Putting care, attention, and love into your cooking will more than make up for any substituted ingredients.

"Keep it simple in the kitchen. If you use quality ingredients, you don't need anything fancy to make food delicious"

- Curtis Stone

The Crimp

If there is a defining feature of a Cornish pasty, it has to be the crimp. It's what separates a pasty from a pie, or a turnover. Quite simply, take away the crimp and it's no longer a pasty!

Like the debate over whether to use the word turnip or swede, the debate about how to crimp a Cornish pasty can get rather lively! Do you crimp down the side, or over the top? Left to right (hen) or right to left (cock)? Should the crimp by big enough to use as a handle, or small and elegant?

Topside

The PGI specifications laid down by the CPA state that Cornish pasties must be crimped "*to one side, and never on top*". While it's true that the vast majority of pasties produced and sold in Cornwall are crimped that way, was that always the case?

Traditionally, crimping on the side or over the top would have been a matter of personal taste. Most likely, your choice of crimp would have depended on the way you were taught by your mother, and so some families would use a top crimp, and others a side crimp. Even today, there are plenty of people top crimping their pasties at home in Cornwall, and there are some pasty shops selling top-crimped pasties. Why then, does the PGI specification insist that a Cornish pasty must be side crimped?

The reason appears to be largely commercial. By trying to keep all Cornish pasties looking more or less the same, it adds a certain amount of 'branding' to the shape. There could also be a production consideration for the bigger businesses in the CPA – I believe it's easier for side crimping to be done by machine, than top crimping (and the PGI specification clearly allows for crimping by machine, where it states that Cornish pasties must be "crimped either by hand or mechanically to one side, and never on top")

But to me, if pasties have been both side crimped and top crimped in Cornwall for hundreds of years, it seems ridiculous that either one or the other method should be chosen arbitrarily. Surely, if a pasty producer has been crimping on top for generations they should continue to do so – in fact, protecting their right to crimp in the traditional way their family has been using for generations would do more to protect the heritage of the Cornish pasty than forcing all producers to use a side crimp! Unfortunately though, the PGI specification does require a side crimp on all products labelled and sold as "Cornish Pasties", and so any pasty makers in Cornwall who crimp on top must now either change to a side crimp, or no longer call their products "Cornish pasties"!

Cock or Hen?

Whether a pasty is crimped from left to right, or right to left depends on the crimper, or more specifically whether the crimper is left handed or right handed.

A right handed crimper will tend to crimp from left to right, creating a hen pasty. A left handed crimper will of course go the other way, right to left, creating a cock pasty. Of course, there are many more right handed people than left handed (roughly 9:1) and so the vast majority of pasties are hens, just as you'd have a single rooster to a dozen or so hens in a chicken shed. So next time you're eating a pasty, take a look at which way the crimp is going – if it's going right to left you're eating a rare pasty!!

Mythology of the Crimp

There are whole plethora of stories about the pasty, and in particular about the crimp. Like most stories, they appear to be grounded in truth, but over the years they have become myths and as such should be taken with a rather large pinch of salt.

The first one being that the purpose of the crimp is as a "handle" for miners to hold their pasties by while eating them, so that their dirty hands wouldn't touch the part of the pasty they are eating (since they would throw the crimp away – more on that in a minute).

Well, lets take a closer look at this idea and see if it holds up. On the face of it, it seems very logical. Miners hands are going to be dirty, and you don't want dirt on your food do you? In fact, worse than "dirt" is arsenic which is notoriously toxic and as a by product of tin and copper mining would have been on the miner's hands a lot of the time (in the late nineteenth century, Cornish mines were producing more than 50% of the World's arsenic!), so avoiding arsenic contamination of their food would have been important.

However, the typical way of carrying a pasty was to have it wrapped in linen, so surely it would be easier and cleaner to simply hold the pasty using the linen wrap, in the same way that one might eat a modern pasty from a paper bag? It seems to me, that would be far more hygienic than trying to hold a pasty by the crimp while avoiding contamination of the rest of the pasty.

There's another reason that I'm skeptical about the crimp-handle theory. If I spend the morning out in the garden, digging over the herb patch for example, by lunchtime I'm ravenous. If I then have a pasty for my lunch, there's no way I'm going to be leaving a single mouthful, let alone the entire crimp. Now I've never worked in a tin mine, but I'm pretty sure that if I did I would be even more hungry at lunchtime than after a morning of pottering about in the garden, so I just can't imagine that miners would have wanted to throw away a portion of their lunch every day just to avoid a little dirt, not when there is a simpler and more efficient way of doing it with the linen wrapper.

Of course, there are arguments the other way. Wheat was expensive and so traditionally pasty crusts would have normally been made with barley flour, which does produce a very tough pastry. I suspect it's more than likely that the crimp was often left until last, and if they were full before eating the whole thing, the remaining crimp would indeed have been thrown away, but suggesting that it was always done, or indeed that the pasty was "designed" with the intention of leaving the crimp in the sake of cleanliness seems a little far fetched to me.

Knockers

We'll never know quite how common it was for miners to throw away the crimp, or part of the crimp, of their pasties but we can be pretty sure it would have happened at least some of the time. And that of course led to another myth – the knockers!

It seems that every culture around the World has invented mythological creatures or figures to try and rationalise the unexplained. The Irish have leprechauns, the Scottish have brownies, and the Cornish have knockers! (There's even a really far fetched but rather famous myth about a man whose mother was a virgin, who was able to turn water into wine and walk on water, and who rose from the dead – amazingly, some people still believe that to this day!)

It's believed that the name comes from the knocking sounds miners would hear on the mine walls before a cave in, a sound of course we now know to be a product of the creaking earth and timbers before giving way. Some miners believed that malevolent spirits lived down the mines and the knocking was the sound of them hammering on the walls, attempting to cause a cave in. Others believed they were the ghosts of miners who had died in previous accidents, and their knocking was a warning.

Either way, a tradition of throwing the final bite of the crimp down into the mine to appease or thank the knockers formed, and this is quite likely to be in some way related to the idea of miners throwing away the crimp to avoid eating food that had been contaminated from holding it with dirty hands.

Just The Facts

As interesting as the colourful stories might be, the simple fact is that the practical reason for the crimp is to seal the pasty. Get the crimp wrong, and the pasty will split and leak juices while baking, and of course there's no denying that the crimp is one of the defining features of the Cornish pasty, so if you're going to be making your own pasties you'll want to get it right!

Crimping Methods

Pasty crimps are a little bit like fingerprints, in fact it's often possible to tell what pasty shop a pasty was bought from purely by looking at the crimp. While the process is rather simple (pinch, pull, fold and tuck) it's surprising how much variety can be achieved.

Unfortunately the only way to get good at crimping is to practice, but on the plus side every time you practice you get to eat another pasty! Here I'll give you two methods to try, my own one handed crimp and a more traditional two handed approach – try them both and see which you prefer, and over time you'll find what works best for you. I don't give a method for top crimping simply because I have always crimped my pasties on the side.

Traditional (Side) Crimp

With the filling on top of the pastry circle, dampen the exposed edge of the pastry with a little water (don't believe people who say you need to use egg wash, that's pure nonsense!)

Gently lift half of the pastry up and over, forming a D shape and bringing the pastry edges together. Press these edges all the way along to seal them, and make sure that the pasty is turned so that the sealed edge is along the top (away from you).

Starting at the left (go the opposite way if you're left handed!) take hold of the edge at the far left with the index finger and thumb of both hands. The left hand pinches and pulls a crimp forward and slightly over the tip of the right thumb. The left thumb then moves to where the left index finger is, as the right hand pulls the start of the next fold over the left thumb tip and feeds it into the left grip, as the left thumb tucks the previous crimp in. This is repeated to the end, where the final crimp is either folded over the top, or tucked underneath depending on personal preference.

It sounds complicated in writing, but follow the illustration and give it a try – with a little practice you'll get there!

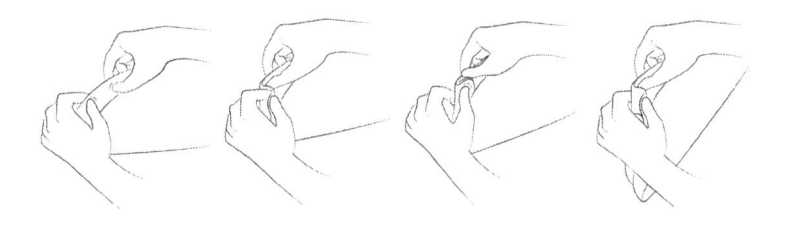

Most pasty makers agree that the number of turns should be somewhere between about 17 and 21 or so.

One Handed (Side) Crimp

Starting in the same way as the traditional crimp, dampen the pastry edge, fold over and press to seal. At this point, I dampen my right index finger and run this quickly along the top edge of the sealed pastry once again (I find this helps the crimp to stay in place).

Starting at the left edge, hold the end of the sealed edge in the right finger and thumb (thumb on top), fold it over onto the sealed edge and push down firmly with the finger. Move to the next section of edge, fold in the same way and repeat all the way to the end. Rather than fold the last crimp over or tuck it under, I fold it onto itself and squeeze it gently with the finger and thumb of both hands to form a small "knob". I normally crimp around 18 turns on my pasties.

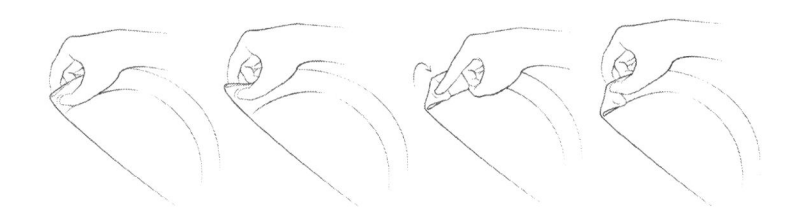

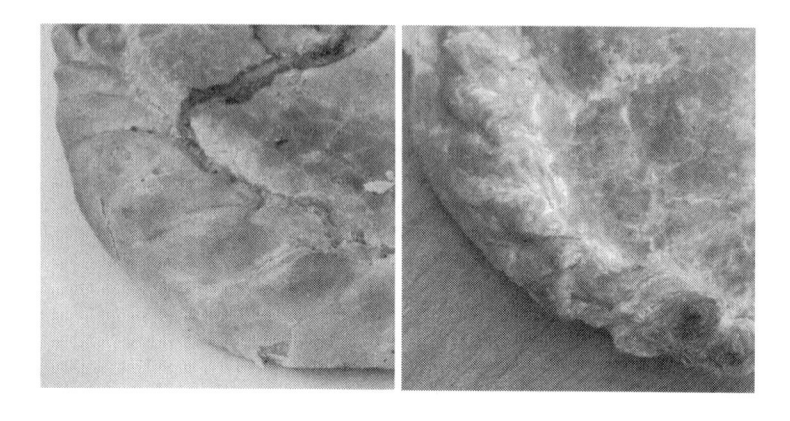

A couple of examples of traditionally crimped pasties.

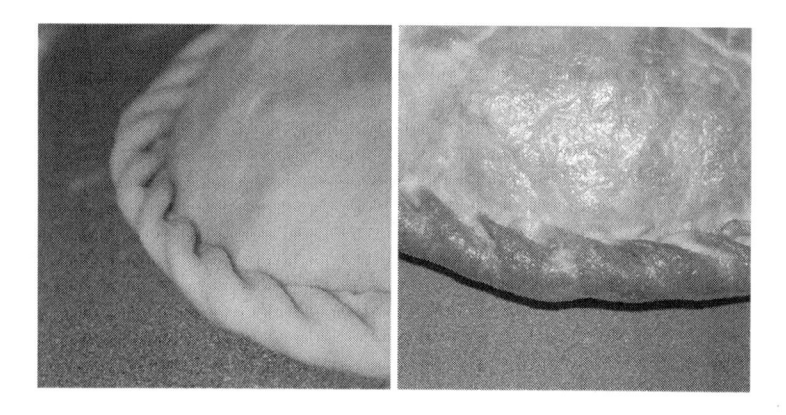

My "one handed" side crimp, on both a raw and cooked pasty. This tends to produce a slightly smaller crimp than is traditional.

An Award Winning Cornish Pasty

This is the exact recipe which won the Amateur Cornish Pasty World Championship title 2 years in a row. As you can see, there are no secret ingredients! Just use good quality ingredients and pay attention to the seasoning (*tip – you probably want to use more pepper than you think!*) and your pasties should turn out just fine.

Makes 4 pasties

For the pastry
525g plain flour
225g vegetable shortening (I use Trex)
3 tsp salt
Cold water (Tip - keep a bottle of tap water in the fridge to use for pastry)
1 egg (for washing)

For the filling
500g beef skirt
2 medium potatoes
2 medium onion
½ small swede
Knob of butter
Salt and pepper

To make the pastry

Place the flour (no need to sift) into a large mixing bowl with the salt and shortening. Rub the fat into the flour until the mixture resembles fine breadcrumbs, and there are no lumps. Now slowly add a little cold water at a time and bring the mixture together until it binds and forms a dough. It's impossible to give an exact amount of water as it will depend slightly on the flour you use, just go slowly and stop when the mixture binds (too much water will make the pastry tough) When a dough forms, knead it briefly for a minute or so, then wrap in cling film and rest in the fridge for 30 minutes while you prepare the filling.

To make the pasties

Preheat the oven to 180°C/350°F/gas 4.

Dice the potatoes, swede, and onions and place them into the mixing bowl you used for the pastry. Add a good pinch of salt, a little shake of white pepper, and a good amount of freshly ground black pepper (really go for it, you'll be surprised how much pepper it needs!) and give it a good mix up with your hands. Trim any excess fat from the beef, then dice it and set aside in 4 equal piles.

Remove the pastry from the fridge and roll out into circles, using a dinner plate as a template. The amount of pastry should be just enough to cut 4 rounds at the right thickness with just a small amount of trimmings.

On each circle place a good handful of the vegetables, then the beef. Add a knob of butter, a pinch of flour (which absorbs excess moisture and thickens the juices) and a little extra salt and pepper since we didn't season the beef.

Now wet along one edge of the pastry with a finger dipped in water, and fold the other side over to encase the filling. Gently press all the way along to form a seal, while gently squeezing out any excess air. Now, crimp the edge all the way along. Personally I always start on the left, and make about 18 crimps finishing in a small knob of pastry on the right.

Crack the egg into a cup with a dash of cold water and a pinch of salt, beat with a fork and brush this all over the pasties (if you want to add initials, now is the time to do so!). Make a steam hold in the middle of each with a sharp knife, and transfer them to greased baking sheets. Bake in the oven for around 50 minutes until they are golden brown, and smelling 'ansome!

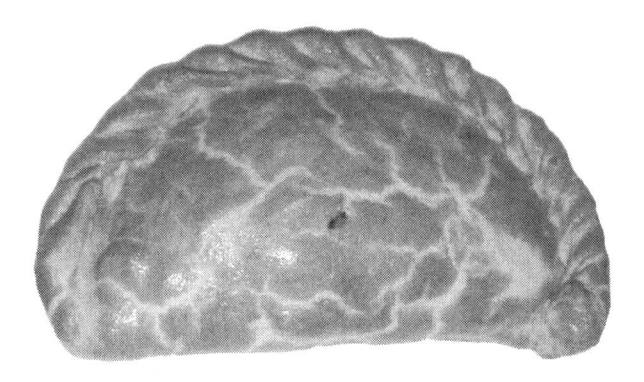

Pasty Pie

I very often make a pasty pie to use up any left over pastry, if I have a little left over but not quite enough to make a pasty. Sometimes I make them from scratch though as a quick and easy, and slightly lighter option than a proper pasty. Since you only have a pastry top, they are a bit healthier (which I think means you can eat more!) but just as tasty.

Here's my recipe for making pasty pie from scratch, which was originally published in The Guardian prior to the 2013 World Pasty Championships - almost as tasty as a proper pasty but a little lighter and incredibly quick and easy to make!

Serves 2

For the pastry

175g plain flour
75g vegetable shortening
1 tsp salt
Cold water
1 egg

For the filling

200g beef skirt
1 medium potato
1 medium onion
½ small swede
Knob of butter
Salt and pepper

In a large bowl, combine the salt and flour, then rub in the fat until the mixture resembles fine breadcrumbs. Then bring together using just enough cold water to bind. Wrap in cling film, and refrigerate for 30 mins.

Preheat the oven to 180°C/350°F/gas 4.

Dice the beef, potato, swede and onion and mix together in a bowl with plenty of salt and pepper. Place the mixture into a pie dish, and add a knob of butter and a light sprinkling of flour.

Roll out the pastry to approximately 3mm thickness, lay over the top of the pie dish, pinch around the edges and trim off the excess. Beat the egg with a little water and a pinch of salt, and brush all over the pastry. Make a couple of small holes for the steam to escape, and bake in the oven for approximately 45 minutes until golden brown.

Pastry Options

For me, a "proper pasty" has to be made with shortcrust pastry. Many will agree with me, though many more won't. In fact, discussions about what sort of pastry is best can get almost as heated as those about what to call a swede!

Visit some of the best pasty makers in Cornwall and you'll find quite a selection of pastries. The Chough Bakery in Padstow, who have won many awards for their delicious pasties use a shortcrust (which of course I heartily agree with!), but there are other very popular and very successful producers using rough puff, or flakey. Some, such as the Horse and Jockey in Porthleven even offer a choice (want a medium flakey and a large shortcrust? No problem!)

Many pasty shops also offer different pastries for different fillings, with a common option being a wholemeal veg (vegetarian pasty in a wholemeal pastry). Now, I realise that this is done for commercial reasons (they obviously figured out that vegetarians are more likely to want a wholemeal crust, while us carnivores tend to prefer our flour lily white) but I would love for that to change. I'd love to be able to buy a wholemeal steak pasty now and then, and I'm sure there are veggies who like a plain white crust... pasty shops, are you listening?

As a side note, a quick warning to the veggies and vegans reading this – just because a pasty shop sells a "vegetable pasty" don't automatically assume that it's suitable for vegetarians. I know of at least one pasty shop here in Cornwall (one that makes damn good pasties by the way!) that sells a "vegetable pasty" and uses lard in the pastry! I'm not going to name any names, but you have been warned!

Of course, we're more interested in home made pasties anyway, which is why I've decided to offer a selection of different pastries so you can mix and match. I've even done my best, at the request of several people, to develop a gluten free recipe so those with a wheat allergy don't have to miss out!

The following recipes each make enough for 4 medium(ish) sized pasties, so feel free to adjust as necessary. If you only want to make 2, just half the quantities (or stop being silly, make 4, and eat the others tomorrow!) If you want to make 8 then double it...

Another note to the veggies – to make vegetarian/vegan friendly versions, simply replace lard with a suitable vegetable shortening, and butter with a suitable margarine.

Shortcrust

This is the standard pastry recipe I use for making pasties, and for pie tops, and is the pastry I used for my award winning pasties. This is a simple to make, great textured, and great tasting pastry which works just as well for sweet as for savoury (you can use this pastry for something like apple pasties, no need to use a specific sweet pastry)

525g plain flour
225g vegetable shortening
1 tsp salt (only use ½ tsp if using with a sweet filling)
Cold water

Place the flour (no need to sift!) into a large mixing bowl, add the salt and the fat and chop the fat into the flour with a knife. Then switch to using your hands, and rub the fat in until the mixture resembles fine breadcrumbs. When all the fat has been rubbed in, slowly add water a little at a time and bring the mixture together into a dough. When a dough has formed, lightly knead for just a minute then form into a ball, wrap in cling film and allow to rest in the fridge for at least 30 minutes before use.

Flakey

450g plain flour
160g lard
160g butter
2 tsp salt
Cold water

Place the flour and salt into a mixing bowl, and rub in half of the lard. Add just enough water to form a dough. Flour a worktop and roll the dough out to form a rectangle about ½cm thick. Mix together the remaining lard and butter. Dot a third of the lard and butter over two thirds of the dough. Fold the third without any fat on it into the middle, covering half of the fat. Then fold the other third on top. Press down on the edges to seal and turn the dough 90 degrees. Chill for ten minutes.

Repeat that last stage 2 more times, using the rest of the lard and butter, chilling again after each folding. Finally roll and fold one final time without adding any fat, and chill for 30 minutes before using.

Wholemeal

225g wholemeal flour
225g strong white flour (bread flour)
100g butter
100g lard
2 tsp salt
Cold water

Place both flours into the bowl. We combine the wholemeal flour with strong flour since wholemeal doesn't have enough gluten to make a pliable pastry. Adding the strong flour which has a higher gluten content makes it much easier to crimp!

As for the shortcrust, chop the fats into the flour and salt, then rub in with your fingers until the mixture resembles fine breadcrumbs. When all the fat has been rubbed in, slowly add water a little at a time (you'll need slightly more water than for shortcrust) and bring the mixture together into a dough. When a dough has formed, lightly knead for just a minute then form into a ball, wrap in cling film and allow to rest in the fridge for at least 30 minutes before use.

Gluten-free

I feel rather sorry for anyone with a wheat allergy. I love bread, and crumpets, and muffins... and buns, baps, baguettes and bagels... not to mention cakes and scones, pasta, pies, and of course pasties! There are of course gluten free versions of most of those, but they aren't nearly as readily available and so I have no doubt that anyone with a wheat allergy misses out on a lot of fantastic food. In fact, I think it's probably one of the worst food allergies to have – with the possible exception of chocolate, chillies, oysters, or beer (not necessarily in that order!)

With that in mind, and knowing several people who are wheat intolerant I really wanted to include a gluten free pasty recipe. Little did I know how difficult working with gluten free pastry could be. As my friend Jon put it "If you can get the pastry somewhere between 'falls apart immediately' and 'sets so hard you can stab people with shards of it', you're doing quite well."

After a lot of research and experimenting, I can say that I have developed a recipe which just about avoids those two extremes, and so I guess I'm doing OK. I have to be honest, this is not the tastiest pastry in the world, the texture doesn't even come close to a nice shortcrust, and it's a real pain to work with. However, if you can put up with with those annoyances, and are willing to put in a bit of time and effort, then this is a way for anyone who is wheat intolerant to enjoy something approaching a "proper pasty"!

Unlike the other pastry recipes, this one is enough for one single pasty since often you'll be only making a single gluten-free pasty for one member of the family and using a different pastry for everyone else. If you want to make more, just multiply the quantities.

150g Doves Farm gluten free plain flour
1 tsp Xanthan gum (available in health food shops)
75g Butter
Pinch of salt
Cold water

Mix the flour, xanthan gum and salt together well, then rub in the butter and form into a dough with the water in the usual way (gluten free flour will absorb a little more water than regular plain flour).

No need to knead as there is no gluten to release, so wrap in cling film and chill for 30 minutes.

When you come to make the pasty, first remember to flour your surface using the gluten free flour not wheat flour! Work slowly – I find that you need to use less pressure with the rolling pin and keep rolling for longer to avoid it cracking. You need to roll it fairly thin otherwise it will be very tough, so take your time and if necessary form the dough back into a ball and start again.

When you've folded the pastry over the filling (being very gentle!) you'll need to modify the crimp. Regular crimping won't work as the pastry isn't pliable enough, so either seal the edges with the tines of a fork like you might do with a turnover, or else press the edges down firmly with your fingers and then simply 'pinch' a crimp into the pastry along the edge. I prefer the second method as it gives a result that looks more like a proper pasty, but you do need to be firm to create a good seal.

Finally, if you struggle with folding and crimping with this pastry, there's no shame in cheating and simply using this to make a pasty pie. Just add the filling to an individual pie dish, roll the pastry out and lay over the top. It will still taste just as good, but is a lot easier to make!

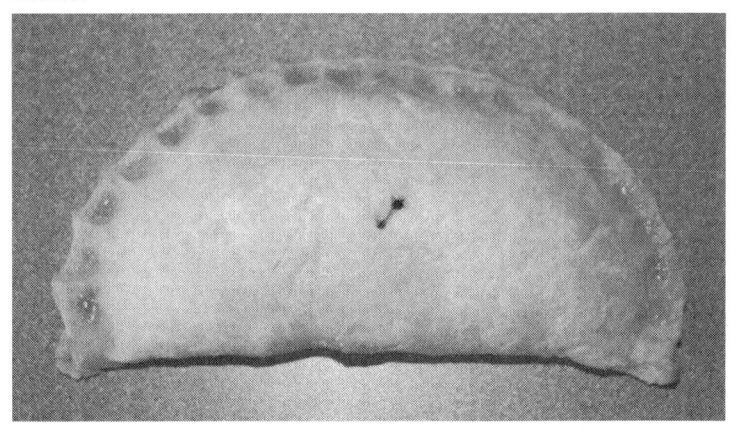

These gluten free pasties won't win any awards for looks, but 'tis better than no pasty at all!

Other Pasty Recipes

The earliest commercial recipe book which deals with pasties, *Cornish Recipes Ancient and Modern* first published in 1929, lists 17 different pasty recipes including such delicacies as broccoli pasty, mackerel pasty, sour sauce pasty, herby pasty, rabitty pasty and windy pasty!

I decided not to call this section "Non-traditional Pasty Recipes" because the idea that a "traditional Cornish pasty" would only contain beef, potato, swede and onion seems to be somewhat of a modern invention. Certainly that combination of ingredients has been massively popular over the centuries and is now firmly rooted as the definitive Cornish pasty, but most sources suggest that historically, Cornish pasties would have been filled with whatever was to hand. In fact, there's an old legend which is also mentioned in the same book:

"It is said that the Devil never crossed the Tamar into Cornwall, on account of the well-known habit of Cornishwomen of putting everything into a pasty, and that he was not sufficiently courageous to risk such a fate!"

Clearly there is precedent for different fillings, and in the coming pages you'll find a collection of recipes to suit any palate. These recipes are inspired from multiple sources: some are quite traditional and some are more contemporary, while some are entirely my own creations. Many of the original sources were extremely lacking in details (for example, one traditional recipe for a lamb and parsley pasty simply reads, "Parsley, and lamb or mutton" - that was the entire recipe!) and so I've tested, tweaked, expanded and modified. I've had a lot of fun testing and experimenting with these, and I hope you'll have fun trying them yourselves, and also making your own adjustments. After all, food should be fun, and everyone's tastes are different so don't be afraid of altering the recipes and making these your own.

Oh, and if you're wondering what a "windy pasty" is, it's a bit of left over pastry, rolled out into a round and folded over, crimped, and baked. Then it's split open while still hot, and filled with jam. And I can confirm it's rather tasty too!

> "I read recipes the same way I read science fiction. I get to the end and say to myself "well that's not going to happen.""
>
> - Rita Rudner

"Mawther used to get a herring, clean 'un, and put same stuffin' as what yow do have in mabiers (chicken); sew 'en up with a niddle and cotton, put 'un in some daugh made of suet and flour; pinch the daugh up in the middle and lave the heid sticking out one end, and tail t'other. They was some nice pasties too, cooked in a fringle fire with crock and brandis and old furzy tobs"

> – Star Gazing Pasties recipe from Cornish Pasties Ancient and Modern, 1929

Other Pasty Recipes

Steak and Blue	77
Steak and Ale	78
Chilli Beef	80
Spiced Oxtail and Sweet Potato	82
Lamb and Mint	84
Pork and Sage	85
Cheese and Bacon	86
English Breakfast	87
Chicken and Mushroom	89
Chicken and Chorizo	91
Roasted Mediterranean Vegetable	92
Roasted Squash, Ricotta and Sage	94
Mushroom and Blue Cheese	96
Tricolore	98
Cheese, Leek and Onion	100
Cheese and Marmite	101
2 Course Pasties	102
Apple Pasties	108
Mince Pie Pasties	110

Steak and Blue Pasties

Makes 4

Your choice of pastry for 4 pasties (See pastry section)

500g beef skirt
2 medium potatoes
2 medium onion
½ small swede
100g blue cheese (Cornish blue works well, as does Stilton)
Salt and pepper
1 Egg

Preheat the oven to 180°C/350°F/gas 4.

Make and bake these using the same method as for traditional Cornish pasties but instead of adding a knob of butter, crumble a quarter of the blue cheese over the top of the filling. The cheese will melt down in with the beef and vegetables and create a lovely rich filling which smells amazing when it comes out of the oven!

Steak and Ale Pasties

Makes 4

Your choice of pastry for 4 pasties (See pastry section)

500g braising steak
100g mushrooms
2 medium onions
½ small swede
1 bottle Cornish ale (Doombar is my current favourite!)
250 ml good beef stock
Spring of thyme
Salt and pepper
2 tsp cornflour
Butter
1 Egg

Preheat the oven to 180°C/350°F/gas 4.

I love a good steak and ale pie – the ultra-tender beef, and the really rich gravy along with the crumbly pastry is a real winning combination. Getting that taste in a pasty however poses a problem, because the gravy is too wet and will make for a soggy pastry!

The key is to cook the meat and then allow it to cool. If the gravy is thick enough it will be almost solid when chilled, giving just enough time for the pastry to start to cook before it melts.

Start by softening a knob of butter in a casserole dish on the stove. Add the diced beef, and allow it to colour on all sides. When the beef is nicely browned on all sides, remove it and set aside, and add the chopped mushrooms, and half of the chopped onions to the same pan. Cook on a medium heat for a few minutes to soften, and then remove them from the pan and set aside with the beef.

Return the pan to the heat, add the ale and deglaze. Add the stock, then return the beef, onions and vegetables to the pan, along with the thyme, and season with salt and lots of black pepper. Place a lid on and put the casserole into the oven for 40 minutes.

Remove the casserole from the oven, remove the thyme sprig and discard, and stir in the cornflour. If the mixture is still quite wet, cook for a few minutes over a low heat with the lid off. Set aside, and when cool enough chill in the fridge for at least an hour.

When you're ready to make the pasties, roll out the pastry in the usual way, and fill with the chopped swede and remaining onion, and the beef mixture which should be quite thick. No need to add a knob of butter, just fold and crimp in the usual way. I cook these in a slightly higher oven than normal at 220°C/425°F/gas 7 for the first 10 minutes to give the pastry a chance to start firming up, then drop the temperature back to 180°C/350°F/gas 4 for another 30 – 35 minutes.

Chilli Beef Pasties

Makes 4

Your choice of pastry for 4 pasties (See pastry section)

500g braising steak
1 can kidney beans
1 can plum tomatoes
1 tbsp tomato puree
1 large onion
1 clove garlic
250 ml good beef stock
1 tsp dried thyme
1tsp chilli powder
½ tsp cumin
Tabasco sauce (optional)
1 tbsp vegetable oil
Salt and pepper
Butter
1 Egg

Tip – making the filling the day before, and then allowing it to chill in the fridge over night works really well for this recipe, and helps to firm up the filling before making the pasties!

Add the oil to a large, heavy based pan over a medium-high heat. Trim and dice the beef, and brown off in the pan, turning until it's coloured on all sides. Remove the beef from the pan and set aside.

Chop the onion and soften in the pan, adding the garlic clove (crushed) after 2 – 3 minutes. When the onion is soft, add the thyme, cumin, and chilli powder and cook for 30 seconds, then add the stock, tomatoes, and tomato puree to the pan, along with the beef that had been set to one side. Season with salt and pepper, turn down to a low heat and cook for 30 minutes, stirring occasionally.

Add the beans, stir well and taste. At this stage you want to adjust the seasoning and the heat (tip – I like to add some Tabasco sauce at this stage until I'm happy with it, but then I like it nice and hot!). If the mixture is still quite wet, leave it to cook a little longer (with the lid off!) until the mixture is thick and there is no excess liquid. Then remove from the heat, and allow to cool.

Preheat the oven to 220°C/425°F/gas 7.

Now proceed to roll out your pastry, and make, crimp and egg wash the pasties in the normal way. Bake them for around 35 – 40 minutes until the pastry is a nice golden brown and, if you have the willpower, allow them to cool a little before tucking in!

Spiced Oxtail and Sweet Potato Pasties

Makes 4

Your choice of pastry for 4 pasties (See pastry section)

750g oxtail
2 large onions
1 large sweet potato
250ml beef stock
2 cloves garlic
1 red or orange capsicum pepper
1 Scotch bonnet pepper (or habanero)
1 lime
½ tsp cumin
½ tin plum tomatoes
1 tbsp vegetable oil
Salt and pepper
Butter
1 Egg

Preheat the oven to 150C/300°F/gas 2.

Place a large, heavy based casserole dish over a high heat, add the oil, brown the oxtail on all sides in batches so as not to over crowd the pan. When the oxtail is nicely browned, set aside. Chop one of the onions and add to the pan, cook for 2 – 3 minutes until starting to soften, then add the cumin, garlic (leave the cloves whole), and chopped peppers (leave the seeds in the Scotch bonnet if, like me, you like a bit of heat!) and stir for a minute before adding the tomatoes and the stock, then return the oxtail to the pan. Halve the lime and add that to the pan, then bring it up to a simmer, cover the pan, and then place in a low oven for 2 hours, turning the oxtail half way through.

Remove the pan from the oven, take out the oxtail and set aside to cool. Pour off any excess fat from the pan, and use a wooden spoon to squash the 2 garlic cloves which will now be very soft. Squeeze the lime halves, and discard the peel. Place the pan over a medium heat, and reduce the liquid until it's nice and thick, scraping the sides and bottom of the pan to get all the sticky brown bits (which add a lot of flavour).

When the oxtail is cool, carefully remove the meat from the bones, roughly chopping it and discarding any fat as you go. When all the meat has been picked from the bones, stir it into the liquid. Taste, and adjust the seasoning and heat if necessary, then cover the pan and allow to chill in the fridge.

Preheat the oven to 220°C/425°F/gas 7.

Peel and chop the remaining onion, and the sweet potato. Roll out the pastry, and fill with the sweet potato, onion, and the oxtail mixture which should now be quite firm. Crimp and egg wash as usual, and bake for around 35 minutes until golden brown.

Lamb and Mint Pasties

Makes 4

Your choice of pastry for 4 pasties (See pastry section)

500g lamb neck
2 medium potatoes
2 medium onion
½ small swede
1 tbsp freshly chopped mint (or 2 tsp dried mint)
Knob of butter
Salt and pepper

Preheat the oven to 180°C/350°F/gas 4.

Follow the recipe for traditional Cornish pasties, the only difference here is using the lamb instead of the beef, and sprinkling the mint over the filling just before crimping – delicious!

> "Good food is the foundation of genuine happiness"
>
> - Auguste Escoffier

Pork and Sage Pasties

Makes 4

Your choice of pastry for 4 pasties (See pastry section)

500g pork tenderloin
2 medium potatoes
2 medium onions
½ small swede
8 large leaves of sage, chopped (or 2 tsp dried sage)
Knob of butter
Salt and pepper

Preheat the oven to 180°C/350°F/gas 4.

Follow the recipe for traditional Cornish pasties, the only difference here is using the pork instead of the beef, and mixing the sage in with the vegetables. I like to use even more black pepper than usual here, it works really well with the pork!

Cheese and Bacon Pasties

Makes 4

Your choice of pastry for 4 pasties (See pastry section)

6 rashers of good quality streaky bacon
200g strong Cheddar cheese, grated
2 medium potatoes
1 medium onion
2 tbsp chopped fresh chives
Salt and pepper

Preheat the oven to 180°C/350°F/gas 4.

Chop the bacon and cook in a dry frying pan for 3 – 4 minutes until nicely coloured, then set aside and allow to cool.

Chop the vegetables as for traditional Cornish pasties, add the bacon, grated cheese, and chives and season well.

Roll out the pastry and fill, crimp, and egg wash the pasties as usual. Bake for 45 – minutes until golden brown. Allow to cool slightly before eating, as the cheese gets very hot!

English Breakfast Pasties

Makes 4

Your choice of pastry for 4 pasties (See pastry section)

4 pork sausages
4 rashers of streaky bacon
3 eggs
100g mushrooms
100g black pudding
Salt and pepper
A little cooking oil
1 extra egg

Add a little oil to a large non-stick frying pan, or a heavy skillet and place on a medium heat. Crack 2 eggs into the pan, and roughly stir with a wooden spoon or spatula to quickly cook. Roughly "chop" the eggs with the wooden spoon, and remove from the pan to cool. Slice the mushrooms and black pudding and add these to the pan, cook for a couple of minutes, turning once. Remove and set aside with the eggs. Turn up the heat and add the sausages to the pan, and cook for a few minutes, just long enough to brown them on all sides. While they are cooking, chop the bacon and add that to the pan with the sausages. When the sausages and bacon are browned, remove from the pan and allow to cool.

When cooled, roughly chop the sausages and black

pudding, combine all the ingredients in a bowl, season well and mix.

Preheat the oven to 220°C/425°F/gas 7.

Roll out your pastry and fill with the mixture you already prepared. Crimp, egg wash and bake as for normal pasties except at a slightly higher heat and for a little less time (since the filling is cooked, you'll only need to leave them in the oven for 35 – 40 minutes)

Enjoy! By the way, this is the ONLY time that it's OK to have baked beans with a pasty!!

> "If you want to eat well in England, you should eat three breakfasts"
>
> - W. Somerset Maugham

Chicken and Mushroom Pasties

Makes 4

Your choice of pastry for 4 pasties (See pastry section)

2 large chicken breasts, skin removed
150g mushrooms
1 clove of garlic, crushed
2 medium potatoes
1 medium onion
1 tsp dried tarragon
1 tbsp vegetable oil
Knob of butter
Salt and pepper

Slice the mushrooms, and fry in a little oil for 2 minutes, add the garlic and fry for another 2 minutes until soft and starting to take on some colour. Remove the pan from the heat, add a pinch of flour and stir in, then set aside to cool.

Preheat the oven to 180°C/350°F/gas 4.

Peel and chop the potato and onion, mix in the cooled mushrooms and tarragon, season well and mix thoroughly. Dice the chicken.

Roll out the pastry and fill with the vegetable mixture, topped with the chicken and a knob of butter. Fold, crimp and egg wash as usual and bake for 45 – 50 minutes.

> "In the abstract art of cooking, ingredients trump appliances, passion supersedes expertise, creativity triumphs over technique, spontaneity inspires invention, and wine makes even the worst culinary disaster taste delicious"

- Bob Blumer

Chicken and Chorizo Pasties

Makes 4

Your choice of pastry for 4 pasties (See pastry section)

2 large chicken breasts, skin removed
150g chorizo
2 medium potatoes
1 medium onion
1 tsp dried thyme
Pinch of smoked paprika
1 tbsp vegetable oil
Knob of butter
Salt and pepper

Preheat the oven to 180°C/350°F/gas 4.

Peel and chop the potato and onion, add the paprika, season well with salt and pepper and mix thoroughly. Dice the chicken and chorizo.

Roll out the pastry and fill with the vegetable mixture, topped with the chicken and chorizo, then sprinkle over the thyme and add a knob of butter. Fold, crimp and egg wash as usual and bake for 45 – 50 minutes.

Roasted Mediterranean Vegetable Pasties

Makes 4

Your choice of pastry for 4 pasties (See pastry section)

1 Large aubergine
2 Large courgettes
2 Red onions
1 Red pepper
1 Yellow pepper
1 small bulb of fennel
2 large tomatoes
3 Cloves garlic
Handful of fresh oregano (or 2 tsp dried)
Olive oil
Salt
Black pepper
1 Egg

Preheat the oven to 220°C/425°F/gas 7.

Peel and roughly chop the onions. Roughly chop the aubergine, courgettes, fennel, and peppers (discarding the seeds) and place all the vegetables into a roasting tray with the peeled (whole) garlic cloves. Scatter over the oregano and season with salt and black pepper. Drizzle all over with olive oil, and then turn the vegetables to coat evenly. Place in the oven and cook for around 25 minutes, turning once, until they are softened and starting to colour. Remove from the oven, discard the garlic, and leave to cool.

Turn the oven down to 180°C/350°F/gas 4.

Deseed and chop the tomatoes, and mix in with the roasted vegetables.

Roll out your pastry rounds, fill, fold and crimp as for normal pasties but without adding any butter. Brush with egg wash, pierce steam holes in the tops, and bake for around 45 minutes until golden brown.

Roasted Squash, Ricotta and Sage Pasties

Makes 4

Your choice of pastry for 4 pasties

1 Large butternut squash
1 Large onion
100g Ricotta
8 Large fresh sage leaves (or 1 tsp dried)
1 Tsp whole cumin seeds
Salt
Black pepper
1 Egg

Preheat the oven to 200°C/400°F/gas 6.

Peel, deseed, and roughly chop the squash. Place it into a small roasting tray, season with salt and pepper, and scatter over the cumin seeds. Drizzle with enough olive oil to coat. Turn the squash over to cover it evenly in the oil and roast in the oven for 30 – 35 minutes until softened and just starting to colour around the edges. Remove from the oven and set aside to cool.

Turn the oven down to 180°C/350°F/gas 4.

Peel and finely chop the onion. Chop the sage. Roll out your pastry rounds.

Fill each pasty with the roasted squash, a handful of the onion, and then top with sage and then ricotta. Fold and crimp as normal, pierce steam holes in the top and brush with egg wash then place in the oven for around 45 minutes until golden brown.

These pasties work especially well with wholemeal pastry!

"I cook with wine, sometimes I even add it to the food"

- W.C. Fields

Mushroom and Blue Cheese Pasties

Makes 4

Your choice of pastry for 4 pasties

500g mushrooms (chestnut mushrooms work well)
100g blue cheese
1 large onion
1 clove garlic
25g butter
1 tbsp plain flour
1 tsp mixed herbs
Salt
Black pepper
1 egg

Slice the mushrooms. Add the butter to a large frying pan, and fry off the mushrooms until softened, adding the crushed garlic for the last minute. Sprinkle the flour over, and stir in to absorb any liquid. Set aside to cool.

Preheat the oven to 180°C/350°F/gas 4.

Peel and finely chop the onion. Roll out your pastry rounds.

Fill each pasty with a combination of onion, and the mushroom mixture. Season, sprinkle over the mixed herbs, and crumble over the blue cheese before folding and crimping. Egg wash and cook as for normal pasties.

Tip – these work really well with a little bacon! Just finely chop a couple of rashers of streaky back bacon and add to the pan at the start, adding the mushrooms just as the bacon starts to colour.

> "Eat food, mostly plants, not too much"
>
> - Sign in at Glastonbury festival

Tricolore (Mozzarella, Basil and Tomato) Pasties

Makes 4

Your choice of pastry for 4 pasties

2 balls of mozzarella
1 medium onion
300g mini plum tomatoes
Good handful of fresh basil
Olive oil
Salt
Black pepper

Preheat the oven to 180°C/350°F/gas 4.

Cut each of the tomatoes in half, and place them cut side up on a roasting tray. Drizzle with a little olive oil, season with salt and then place into the oven for 25 minutes or until they have shrivelled to about half their original size but not started to burn. This intensifies their flavour, and reduces the moisture content. Remove from the oven and set aside to cool.

Turn the oven up to 220°C/425°F/gas 7.

Slice the mozzarella and pat dry on kitchen towel. Chop the onion.

Roll out the pastry. Fill each pasty with a little of the

onion topped with the tomatoes, then some of the torn basil leaves and then lay slices of mozzarella over the top. Season with black pepper, then fold, crimp and egg-wash in the usual way.

Bake for around 35 minutes until golden brown, and allow to cool slightly before eating as the cheese gets very hot!

"I think preparing food and feeding people brings nourishment not only to our bodies but to our spirits. Feeding people is a way of loving them, in the same way that feeding ourselves is a way of honouring our own createdness and fragility"

- Shauna Niequist

Cheese, Leek and Onion Pasties

Makes 4

Your choice of pastry for 4 pasties

300g strong Cheddar cheese, grated
2 medium potatoes
1 medium onion
1 medium leek
1 clove of garlic
Pinch of cayenne pepper
Salt and pepper

Peel and chop the potatoes, onion, and leek and place into a mixing bowl. Finely slice the garlic and add that to the vegetable mixture, along with the grated cheese. Season with salt and pepper, add a pinch of cayenne pepper, and mix thoroughly.

Preheat the oven to 180°C/350°F/gas 4.

Roll out your pastry rounds, fill with the cheese and vegetable mixture, and then fold and crimp in the usual way. Brush with egg wash and cook as for normal pasties for around 45 minutes, until they are golden brown. Let them cool slightly before eating as the cheese will be very hot!

Cheese and Marmite Pasties

Makes 4

Your choice of pastry for 4 pasties (See pastry section, I think these work best with a wholemeal crust)

300g strong Cheddar cheese, grated
3 medium potatoes
1 medium onion
Marmite
Salt and pepper
1 egg

Preheat the oven to 180°C/350°F/gas 4.

Chop the vegetables as for traditional Cornish pasties, add the grated cheese, and season well.

Roll out the pastry and spread a little marmite over each round, covering the area where the filling normally goes and going into the crimp area (gives a nice, savoury, marmite taste to the crimp!)

Fill the pasties with the cheese and vegetable mixture, then crimp, and egg wash the pasties as usual. Bake for 45 – 50 minutes until golden brown. Allow to cool slightly before eating, as the cheese gets very hot!

I hope you love 'em, but if not you'll probably hate 'em!

"Afters Pasties" & Adventures in TV Land

After winning my second Cornish Pasty Championship title I started getting calls and emails from various people asking if I would be interested in various projects ranging from baking pasties to sell at a farmer's market, to filming a series of "how to" style videos for a local new media TV channel. I turned most of the offers down due to being far too busy with other projects, but there was one offer which caught my attention.

One day I received an email, out of the blue, from a TV producer asking if I'd be interested in working with them. They were in the early stages of planning for the next series of a popular Channel 4 programme, and were looking for someone to work with developing and filming some pasty recipes. The programme was *River Cottage* and since Hugh Fearnely-Whittingstall has always been one of my "food heroes" I jumped at the chance. I knew how stressful television filming can be after competing on TV's Masterchef 2 years running, but I also knew that it was a lot of fun, that I was sure to learn loads from the experience, plus it would be great publicity for this book.

Over the course of several weeks I spoke with the production team on the phone, sent emails back and forth and worked on several recipe ideas. They seemed all set to arrange a date for filming in early July, since I would be at the Glastonbury festival at the end of June, and by coincidence the producer and several of his team were going to Glastonbury too. However, a few days after the festival I had one final email thanking me for all my help, hoping we could work together in the future, but unfortunately they had changed their plans and decided to shoot the piece at a local bakery instead as it would give them a better location to film.

Needless to say I was a little disappointed as it would have been an interesting experience, and by that time I had already invested considerable time and effort into the project. All wasn't lost however, since I'm now able to share one of the recipes I developed for the programme with you...

Pork, onion and sage at one end, fruit at the other

Developing a Two Course Pasty

The concept for the piece was to go "head to head" with Hugh, each of us creating a 2 course "afters" pasty (savoury at one end, sweet at the other) in a little competition. The 2 course pasty is somewhat legendary, with some sources claiming it was very common while others suggest that they were rarely, if ever produced. The idea of course is that you start eating from the savoury end, and when you reach the sweet filling at the other that becomes your "afters".

The only recipes I've been able to find for two course pasties are modern, claiming to be recreations of historical recipes. The earliest work in my collection of books which mention pasties (*Cornish Recipes Ancient and Modern*, first published in 1929) lists no less than 18 different pasty recipes, yet makes no mention of a 2 course pasty (I use the word 'recipe' loosely here - while some of them are more verbose one are two are a little light on details. For example, the recipe for Date Pasty simply reads "Stone dates and fill in the usual way"!) There is lots of evidence however that pasties with sweet fillings, such as apple or jam, were common and so I find it unlikely that two course pasties wouldn't have been experimented with at least on occasion.

In all of the modern two course recipes I found there was a common theme – a barrier of some kind (sometimes using a "flap" of pastry, other times using some stale bread) to keep the sweet and savoury fillings separate.

The idea for the programme was that Hugh would create a pasty using that method, while I would go with a barrier-less pasty. By carefully selecting the fillings, my idea was that it should be possible to create a flavour combination which works even when two fillings mix. I came up with several ideas; venison and blueberry, duck and cherry, and pork and apple.

Pork and apple seemed to work best, not only for the flavour but also texture – if the fruit filling is too wet or soft it will break down during cooking, and can ruin the texture and make the pastry soft. Apple of course works great in pasties and pies, and is a classic flavour combination with pork. So, without further ado, here is the two course pork and apple pasty I created (and do watch out for the next series of River Cottage which as far as I know will still include a two course pasty segment – I'm looking forward to trying Hugh's recipe myself and seeing how it compares to my own!)

Two Course Pork & Apple Pasties

Makes 4 pasties

Ingredients

Your choice of pastry for 4 pasties (See pastry section)

400g pork tenderloin
4 rashers unsmoked streaky bacon
1 medium onion
1 large potato
1 piece of swede (similar size to the onion)
1 large Bramley apple
1 large Braeburn apple
2 tbsp fresh sage (finely chopped)
4 tsp blackcurrant jam
Black pepper
Salt
Butter
A little extra flour
1 egg

Method

Preheat the oven to 180°C/350°F/gas 4.

Chop the bacon into small pieces and fry off in a dry non-stick pan until browned, this gives a nice extra hit of flavour. Dice the pork and set aside. Dice the vegetables as you would for a standard pasty and add the bacon and sage, a couple of good pinches of salt and lots of black pepper, and mix together thoroughly.

Peel, core and chop the apples and set aside. Roll out the pastry into rounds as you would for standard pasties. On each round, place a pile of the vegetables at one end and top with a quarter of the pork (and remember which end is which!). Place a pile of apple at the other end and then a spoonful of jam at the very end. Add a knob of butter and a pinch of flour, then fold and crimp as for standard pasties.

Make holes in the top for the steam to escape, brush with eggwash, and transfer to baking sheets. Bake in the oven for approximately 50 minutes until piping hot and golden brown.

Start eating from the savoury end, and enjoy first a lovely pork and sage pasty which slowly gets a hint of apple, through pork and apple and finally into apple and blackberry.

Two course pasties might not be all that authentic, and even if they were I'm sure this is not the method most people would have used, but they sure are fun to make and to eat so do try them!

Apple Pasties

Makes 10 - 12

Shortcrust pastry, quantity for 4 pasties (See pastry section)

1kg Bramley apples
100g golden caster sugar
½ tsp cinnamon
Knob of butter
Milk to brush
Icing sugar to dust

The standard quantity of pastry for 4 medium pasties will make around 10 - 12 mini dessert pasties, depending on how thinly you roll the pastry, and what size you make your circles.

Preheat the oven to 180°C/350°F/gas 4.

Peel, core, and chop the apples and place them in a mixing bowl. Add the castor sugar and cinnamon and mix well.

Roll out the pastry into small circles, place the apple filling onto each along with a small knob of butter, then fold and crimp in the usual way. Crimping mini pasties can be a little fiddly, especially if you have large fingers, but take your time and they should turn out quite neat.

Make small steam holes in the top of each pasty, brush with milk, and then place on a baking tray. Bake for around 30 minutes. Cool on a wire rack, and then dust with icing sugar before serving.

These are delicious eaten as they are, hot or cold, but are also great with clotted cream! In the summer, you can also add a few blackberries along with the apple, or try experimenting – how about toffee apple, or maybe try cherries, or apricot, or pecans and maple syrup... the possibilities are endless!

Mince Pie Pasties

Makes 10 - 12

Shortcrust pastry, quantity for 4 pasties (See pastry section)

1 jar of mince meat
2 eating apples (such as Breaburn)
Milk to brush
Icing sugar to dust

Preheat the oven to 180°C/350°F/gas 4.

Peel, core, and chop the apples.

Roll out the pastry into small circles, place a little chopped apple on each round and then a spoonful of mince meat, then fold and crimp in the usual way.

Make small steam holes in the top of each pasty, brush with milk, and then place on a baking tray. Bake for around 25 - 30 minutes. Cool on a wire rack, and then dust with icing sugar before serving.

These are always a talking point at Christmas. No matter how bored people are of mince pies, everyone seems to love these mini Christmas pasties. Eat them cold just as they are, or warm with either clotted cream or rum butter – or both!

Appendices

1. Recommended pasty shops

I've spent a lot of time travelling around sampling pasties all over Cornwall trying to find the best ones (yeah I know, it's a tough job but someone has to do it!)

I don't claim to have tried them all, and different people have different tastes so please don't take this as gospel, but if you want to buy a good pasty here is a list of some great places to try...

The Chough Bakery, Padstow

Horse and Jockey, Porthleven

Village Butchers, Mylor Bridge

The Count House Cafe, Geevor Mine

Ann's Pasties, The Lizard

Philp's, Hayle
Be careful – Philp's bakery sell pasties made with minced beef (just plain wrong if you ask me) so make sure you ask for steak!

Portreath Bakery, Portreath

Malcolm Barncutt's, Bodmin

Portreath Bakery, Portreath

2. Pasty Making Tips

Good food starts with good ingredients, so buy the best produce you can find and don't try to penny pinch – the results will be worth it.

Don't rush. I believe anyone can make a great pasty if they take the time to do it properly. Rush and you won't get the results you want, but with a bit of patience, care and attention your pasties will be 'ansome.

Don't put carrot in your Cornish pasties – ever!

Allow the pastry to rest. Don't try and roll out your pastry as soon as you've made it – let it rest in the fridge for AT LEAST 30 minutes first. You can even make it the day before to save time.

Try to keep the crimp small and neat – nobody wants to bite into a huge lump of pastry.

Experiment – unless you're setting up shop to sell Cornish pasties to PGI specifications there are no rules, so adjust the quantities to suit your palate, or experiment with different fillings and pastries.

No carrots! (seriously)

A pasty is a meal in itself, so please don't go serving them with chips and beans – 'tis blasphemy!

Season well, and remember that you'll almost always need to use more pepper than you think!

Have fun. This is really the most important thing, food should be enjoyable so don't stress. If your first attempt doesn't go quite to plan just try again, if the pastry cracks in the oven who cares – it will still taste good. Just relax, and enjoy baking your pasties as much as eating them, and if all else fails open a nice Cornish ale and sup on that while you're baking – that always helps!

And finally, just in case I forgot to say, do not ever include carrots!!!

> "There is no sincerer love than the love of food"
>
> - George Bernard Shaw

3. Further Reading

Books

Cornish Recipes Ancient and Modern, Edith Martin (1929)

The Pasty Book, Hettie Merrick (1995)

The Cornish Pasty, Stephen Hall (2001)

The Official Encyclopedia of the Cornish Pasty, Les Merton (2003)

Pasties, Lindsay Bareham (2008)

The Little Book of the Pasty, Emma Mansfield (2011)

Online

Cornish pasty PGI specifications (COUNCIL REGULATION (EC) No 510/2006 on Protected Geographical Indication)
https://www.gov.uk/government/uploads/system/uploads/attachment_data/file/218651/cornish-pasty-pgi.pdf

The Cornish Pasty Association
http://www.cornishpastyassociation.co.uk

The Eden Project (home of the Cornish Pasty World Championships)
http://www.edenproject.com

The Compleat Pastypaedia
http://www.cornishpasties.org.uk

About The Author

Billy Deakin is a videogame developer and entrepreneur, founding Kernow Web Designs in 2003. He has always had a passion for food and for cooking. He appeared on TV's Masterchef in both 2008 and 2009, and won his first Cornish Pasty World Championship title at the inaugural competition in 2012, successfully defending it in 2013. Billy has also published recipes online under the pen name Judith Stone.

Contact Billy at *billy@properpasties.com*

Photo credits

Poldice mine, page 12
Cousin Jack's pasty shop, page 18
Top crimped pasty, page 24
Pasty tax (Sun newspaper), page 30
Butte pasty and gravy, page 39
Empanadas salteñas, page 40
Swede, page 49
Turnip, page 49
Pasty crimp, page 60 (top left)

GFDL/Eva Kröcher
Flickr/Suzi Rosenberg
Flickr/Mike_fleming
Flickr/Dullhunk
Rachel Boschman
Wiki Commons/Gorivero
Wiki Commons/Magnus Manske
Wiki Commons/Barracuda1983
Wiki Commons/Smalljim

All other images © Billy Deakin, 2013

"Vegetarians, and their Hezbollah-like splinter faction, the vegans ... are the enemy of everything good and decent in the human spirit"

- Anthony Bourdain, Kitchen Confidential

Made in the USA
Charleston, SC
14 October 2013